The Blessing Effect

How Blessing is Changing the World

Richard Brunton

The Blessing Effect
How Blessing is Changing the World
Published by Richard Brunton Ministries
New Zealand

© 2020 Richard Brunton

ISBN 978-0-473-53141-6 (Softcover)
ISBN 978-0-473-53142-3 (ePUB)
ISBN 978-0-473-53143-0 (Kindle)
ISBN 978-0-473-53144-7 (PDF)

Editing:
Special thanks to
Joanne Wiklund and Andrew Killick

Production & Typesetting:
Andrew Killick
Castle Publishing Services
www.castlepublishing.co.nz

Cover design:
Paul Smith

CONTENTS

FOREWORD

Richard's first book, *The Awesome Power of Blessing*, took us to a place that changed our language and caused us to begin speaking Life. He encouraged us to use our God-given authority to bless others and ourselves, and to release the life-changing power of our tongues in order to give glory to God.

This new book, *The Blessing Effect*, is about the results of that knowledge and how we can take blessing to the next level.

I have walked this message with Richard from the beginning as we have travelled and spoken together around the world. We have had many adventures, but a particular example springs to mind. Richard and I travelled to Fiji and ministered to a group of Bible students. After sharing the blessing message, we sent them out to put their new tools into practice. The students returned an hour later, full of joy and with amazing testimonies. As a result, we were asked to bless the entire police force in the area, lined up on parade! So I can testify, from firsthand experience, that what you read here can dramatically change your world – as it has mine.

This book goes beyond the basics of blessing, showing us how God can heal our wounds. As we go through life, events and people can wound us on the inside, but the love and grace of God is there for each of us. My prayer is that you will take hold of your healing, believing the Psalmist when he said that our Heavenly Father '...forgives our iniquities and heals our diseases' (Psalm 103:3).

The testimonies contained in *The Blessing Effect* will encourage and inspire you; and, may I suggest, what God did for others He will do for you! This is a small book, easy to read and simple to apply, but with mighty potential. Write down some action points as you read, then go and change your world.

Pastor Geoff P. Wiklund
Friend in Ministry

Having authored the widely-read book, *The Awesome Power of Blessing,* Richard Brunton has now written this most incisive and appealing treatise, *The Blessing Effect.*

Reading this new book, I am convinced, by the many testimonies, that blessing is indeed changing the world. I am especially thrilled that Richard has included a review of his first book, which will encourage people to read it and, being such a valuable resource, it is advisable to do so. I have personally read it eight times, and I'm now inspired to re-read it a ninth time!

The Blessing Effect highlights incredible stories of people who have applied 'blessing principles' to situations in their own lives or in the lives of others – regardless of cultural background – and have seen profound results. These principles will be the building blocks of faith and hope for many who read this book.

Richard has also explained the principle of the 'Father's Blessing', along with testimonies of people who have received this blessing from either their biological parent or a 'father figure'. I, and many others, have witnessed its tremendously far-reaching effects.

I can vouch for the fact that *The Blessing Effect* is a powerful resource for pastors and leaders. This must-read book should be studied more than read, and I am sure that once you start, you won't stop reading it page by page until you come to the end. It has been given to us as a gift from God through his servant, and will have a great impact upon the lives of the countless numbers who read it. I can't wait to see it printed and distributed, as *The Awesome Power of Blessing* has been, in many countries around the world.

I bless this masterpiece of work in the name of the Father, Son and the Holy Spirit. Amen.

Bishop Michael Musale
General Overseer of Christ Victory Gospel Ministries
President of Victory Christian School
Kenya

The simple step by step wisdom in this book helped me see how easy it is to turn everyday confession from cursing to blessing, over myself, my family and others. The testimonies are powerful and authentic, and encourage and inspire hope for any situation.

Pastor Vivian Anson
New Zealand

I wholeheartedly congratulate Brother Richard Brunton for writing this remarkable book for the Body of Christ. Brother Richard is a compassionate, humble and profound conference speaker with deep insight as an ambassador for Christ. I strongly believe the message of this book answers the basic need of our present age. With the guidance of the Holy Spirit, the writer has given us Bible-rooted principles and made them easy for us to follow and practise. This beautiful book contains revelation of heavenly, spiritual and temporal blessings.

Pastor Sarwar Masih
Pakistan

INTRODUCTION

When I wrote and published my first book, *The Awesome Power of Blessing*, I had high hopes for what it might achieve in the world. I had seen the effects of blessing in my own life and in the lives of others, and wanted to share the message more widely. It spread like wildfire. The Holy Spirit moved, and I just tried to keep up! The book became an unofficial bestseller in New Zealand and, as of June 2020, there are 1.4 million copies, in 35 languages, circulating around the globe.

As the message spread, I began to receive many testimonies about real-life situations changed by blessing. These amazing stories form the basis of this new book, giving readers a greater insight and vision about how blessing can change them, their world and indeed the whole world. Over half of this book has been written by people who have been person-ally impacted by blessing – either as a 'blessee', a 'blessor' or both. I have corrected a few grammatical errors and abridged some of the stories, but otherwise, the style of expression is original and authentic.

Although this booklet can be read as a 'stand-alone', it is really a sequel to *The Awesome Power of Blessing*. That book covers the theory and 'how to' of blessing. It is a practical guide with numerous examples of blessings that can be used in various situations. This book, on the other hand, is primarily focused on the *result* of blessing – *The Blessing Effect* – and how blessing is changing the world, little by little. By including sections on the Father's Blessing, Healing the Wounds of the Heart and the Language of Blessing, I have endeavoured to give this book a practical aspect as well.

In **Part One: The Basics of Blessing**, I give a brief overview of *The Awesome Power of Blessing* for those who haven't read it, as well as refreshing the memory of those who have. This section contains new testimonies that serve to illustrate, in greater depth, some aspects of the first book.

Part Two: The Powerful Effect of a Parent's Blessing explores the significance and power of parental blessings – especially the Father's Blessing. This blessing attracts more testimonies than any of the others – it seems to impact peoples' spirits (and often their bodies as well) in a unique way. I have seen many adults weep as I have spoken a Father's Blessing over them. Many have never heard their father say the words 'I love you', and some have never had a father's loving hug. I estimate that over 95 percent of adults have never been blessed by their father – Christian or not. These days, more children are raised in fatherless homes (one in five in New Zealand), so the problem is only increasing. Some call 'fatherlessness' a modern-day plague, and I agree.

My heart's desire is that every father reading this book will begin to bless their children and their grandchildren. More than that, I hope that fathers will find it in their hearts to bless the 'fatherless', as opportunities arise. I will show you how.

I also give some examples of the power of a Mother's Blessing.

Part Three: The Powerful Effect of Blessing the Body.
As I began to receive testimonies in response to *The Awesome Power of Blessing*, I was surprised at how many were about physical healing and deliverance. Sometimes this comes about because the healing of the heart results in the healing of the body – one just follows the other. Other times, it occurs because someone blesses their body directly and intentionally, with gratitude.

I have come to believe that our bodies respond when we love and affirm them. Many of us have spoken negative words over our bodies – perhaps during our teen years or later as our bodies have changed in undesirable ways. One testimony I received told of a pastor who blessed his body to lose weight – he had lost 37 kilograms.

Part Four: The Powerful Effect of Blessing a Wounded Heart. While parental wounds are often the most significant source of emotional damage in our lives, there are other sources as well, such as cruel and unjust words spoken over us at school, at work, or even in church. These wounds also need healing, and I propose a method for doing that in this section.

Some people feel they are being weak if they can't simply 'get over it' and suppress or move past their pain. However, without the Spirit's intervention, they usually fail to achieve the intimacy and love of God that their heart craves.

Wounds stop us from coming into our destiny as sons and daughters of God and keep us 'lovesick'. We were made for love. When we are able to receive the love of God, we can then give and receive it from others as well.

The love of God changes how we see Him and how we see ourselves. It leads to the enjoyment of God and our ministry to Him and others.

Part Five: The Language of Blessing. The second to last section contains a short but valuable chapter on the Language of Blessing, as I know many people struggle with this aspect of the blessing process. I have also included some brief advice on how to relate to others in your blessing ministry – especially when you are relating to strangers.

Final Word. The book concludes with a blessing for the reader, and information on how to become a Christian.

Enjoy.
Richard Brunton

PART ONE:

The Basics of Blessing

BLESSING:
A REVIEW AND UPDATE

Put simply, *blessing* is the act of speaking words of life (words that build up) over someone or some situation, while *cursing* is the speaking of words of death (words that are critical, discouraging or hurtful). These words impact both the natural world in which we live and the invisible supernatural world that surrounds us.

When people bless or curse in everyday situations, their words naturally carry a certain level of power. So, for example, a father could say to his son, 'You'll never amount to anything,' and that sets a curse in motion that will affect the course of the boy's life. Or he could say, 'Son, I believe you will be a great leader one day,' and these words are a blessing that positively influences the son's future. This is true whether you are a Christian or not. Words are especially powerful when they come from people in authority, such as parents, schoolteachers, managers, doctors and pastors.

However, there is a supernatural component too. A witchdoctor, for example, will speak words of death with the power of Satan behind them and, as a result, people can get sick and even die.

But – and here's the revelation – Spirit-filled Christians can speak God's intentions and favour over someone or some situation, in the name of Jesus or the Trinity (Father, Son and Holy Spirit), and activate the Kingdom of God on earth. They can expect God to change things from the way they are now, to the way He wants them to be.

Blessing others activates God's love and power (and I believe to a greater degree than just prayer alone). Too often we ask God to move the mountain, whereas He has told *us* to speak to the mountain. Or we ask *God* to do something we know is in His will, whereas God wants *us* to speak and release it. As Christians, we carry the Kingdom of God within us and we are meant to release it in the name of Jesus.

For example, we can ask God to give His peace to somebody, or we can simply release it: 'I bless you with the peace of Christ; I release it now in Jesus' name.' This activates our partnership with the Holy Spirit. Our part is to speak and release the blessing; God's part is to perform it (and to stir us to bless in the first place).

That's it. Simple – but with big implications!

At the end of his second letter to the Corinthians, Paul blesses the church:

> *The grace of the Lord Jesus Christ, and the love of God, and the communion of the Holy Spirit be with you all. Amen. (2 Corinthians 13:14)*

The word translated here as 'communion', or 'fellowship' in other translations, is *koinonia*, which can also be translated 'partnership'.

There are several requirements for powerful blessing (*The Awesome Power of Blessing* discusses these in more detail). The big one is that we change our wording from 'God bless so and so' to '*I* bless so and so, in the name of the Father and of the Son and of the Holy Spirit', or simply in the name of Jesus.

When we partner with the Holy Spirit, and move in the spiritual authority that Jesus gained for us on the cross, things really start to happen. When we bless people in the name of Jesus or the Trinity, intentionally and specifically, then God's love and power are released. An amazing privilege! Usually both the person speaking the blessing and the one receiving it are aware that something divine has taken place.

Another important aspect for effective blessing is to have a clean mouth (see Isaiah 6:5-7). Blessing and cursing should not come from the same person (James 3:10). Don't expect God to empower only the words of life you speak and not the words of death. We need to have a mouth that God can trust.

The Awesome Power of Blessing explores the practical aspects of how to bless, addressing various specific situations:

- Blessing your enemies
- Blessing yourself – mind, imagination, body
- Blessing your home
- Blessing your family – spouse, children, and grandchildren
- Blessing the land
- Blessing your community
- Blessing God

Over the last few years, I have blessed many people – in New Zealand, Fiji, Kenya, Uganda, Tanzania, Pakistan and Brazil – both one-on-one and en masse in churches and conferences. I've found that pastors who love the blessing message (some even running blessing seminars and forming blessing groups or 'cells') are seeing the same, or even better, results.

I have found that as I open my heart towards others to bless them, I usually experience God's love flowing through me and often end up in tears myself. I have found that the more I give God's love away, the more of it I have. We grow in love by giving it away! That's how it works.

If we want God to work through us in power – in healing, miracles and deliverance – then we need to operate out of His love and compassion. Faith is activated and energised by God's agape love (Galatians 5:6). Faith flourishes when we know the One who is love and realise how much He loves us and the person to whom we are ministering.

Blessing has changed my life more than any other Christian practice. I have come to know and receive more love, and operate in more power, than ever before. We need to learn the art of being selfless. When we 'lose' our life, that's when we find it (Matthew 10:39). If you want to reach a higher level of experiencing the love and power of God, then blessing is for you.

OVERCOMING OFFENCE:
BLESSING THOSE WHO PROVOKE, HURT OR CURSE YOU

I love the healing ministry – indeed, in some ways I see it as a subset of the blessing ministry. In the healing and deliverance ministries, we speak to the sickness or demon and command it to leave in the name of Jesus. We then release the power of Jesus. Again it's a glorious partnership: our job is to speak and/or lay hands; Jesus does the healing.

Sometimes people come for healing, but they are holding bitterness in their hearts. When they forgive and bless the person who has offended them, then healing comes.

I remember one occasion when a group of people were trying to minister deliverance to a man in a church meeting, but they ran out of time and the job was unfinished. The baton was passed to me, so I took the man to a private place with two others so the meeting could continue undisturbed. I asked him if his father had ever laid hands on him and blessed him.

'No,' he replied.

'May I stand in your father's shoes to give you the blessing you never had?' I asked.

Yes, he was agreeable to that.

When I came to the part where, speaking in the place of his father, I asked for forgiveness for things I had said and done that had hurt him, he replied, 'No.'

Pausing, I asked him about this.

'He used to beat me,' the man explained, 'one time so badly I ended up in hospital. I can't forgive him.'

As I knew that this was going to be the key to everything else, I gently persisted and eventually he made the decision to forgive his father. Immediately he dropped to his knees weeping, and I encouraged him to speak a blessing on his father. The demons then left without further trouble as they no longer had any right to torment him.

Imagine your unforgiveness shown in the form of a bank account. Being able to forgive will take you from a position of overdraft, back to zero. But blessing comes on top of that – it actually puts something *into* the account, and that's when things really begin to happen.

I was bullied at school. One particular boy constantly picked on me. One day, a couple of years later, I went to his house to play. While I was there, his stepfather humiliated him. I now understand that hurt people hurt others. Knowing that fact makes it much easier to bless those who seek to hurt you and move away from seeing yourself as a victim.

I remember reading about a pastor who was angry at God for 'allowing' a man to molest and murder a young girl. He had a dream in which he saw a little child locked in a wardrobe, terrified and crying in the dark.

'There!' he said to God, 'The man's a monster; he's at it again!'

Then God gently spoke, 'The child in the wardrobe is the murderer.'

The pastor wrote that he has never judged anyone since. Nor have I.

Blessing can break down the most difficult of situations. I received this testimony from a soldier in Uganda:

> *I've started praying and blessing seriously my enemies; now my enemies are becoming my friends.*

Pastor Sammy in the Democratic Republic of Congo related:

> *Truly… blessing has a power that can change the world. A man's wife left him with their two daughters without saying a word more than a year ago. He testified to me that he forgave his*

wife and blessed her. Miracles happened: physical healing, spiritual healing, joy filled him and inner peace. Hallelujah.

We know how bitterness can imprison us, but Jay wrote to me saying:

Some of the people I know well have shared with me how they have been released from bitterness towards others as they have started to bless them.

A prison chaplain said:

I have the joy of taking Bible studies in the prison and have distributed your book on the Awesome Power of Blessing. One inmate told me he has read the book more than once. It has changed his whole behaviour. Instead of complaining and grumbling about things and conditions, he now blesses instead. He decided to bless one of the bullies. This guy used to kick him off the phone and give him a hard time. Since blessing him, this guy now protects him while he is on the phone and no longer pushes him off. The result is that both of them are happier.

From a youth pastor in Nepal:

I had the opportunity to read the Nepali version of The Awesome Power of Blessing. *After reading this book, my life has changed dramatically. I remember the time when I got saved in my Hindu family. They were very cruel and cold to me. The way I had been treated by my family, I had never been able to forgive them up to now, but after reading this blessing book, I forgave them. It was a hard process but I am able to bless them now. I feel like my entire burden has been removed from my life. Thank you for providing me the book and changing my world.*

A NEW WAY OF LIVING

As a result of reading *The Awesome Power of Blessing*, and putting it into practice, many people have changed how they live and have adopted a blessing lifestyle. We see that in the following testimonies:

> My sister-in-law gave me a copy of your book, The Awesome Power of Blessing. **It has changed my life.** I have been blessing my wife, my family, my business, my clients, my competitors, and others who don't like me.

Another person writes:

> I'm in a music ministry and gave the book to the band leader, and we discuss it every Wednesday. We liken 'blessing' to pouring water on parched land and, as we are conduits of God's love, we become like hoses pouring water on hotspots. Better still, your message gives us God's super

*weapon of love to **take the offensive** at a time
when we, as God's kids, have been feeling defensive for so long.*

What an insight! Many of us can identify with being
on the back-foot, grimly holding onto a defensive
stance, hoping for victory and so often not seeing it –
but blessing takes the offensive! We fight with God's
weapon and then (not surprisingly) see results.

Natalie writes:

*On a day that I was feeling really low because
of unfair criticism directed at me in the office, I
saw your blessing book and the other little booklet about the workplace (Anointed for Work). I
decided to put the message into practice, and
the power of blessing has **changed the way
I pray and think**. Now I do these things with a
new kind of understanding and faith, using
God-given authority. This truth is so powerful
I ordered 20 books for my Christian friends…
Blessings for new revelations.*

Deborah says:

> The Awesome Power of Blessing *has **changed me at my core** – it has changed what I think about as I wake up, my attitude to my body and illness, and is changing my family and friends… All in all, what you have released here in our town in Queensland, Australia, is literally His river of grace and mercy like a flood. Thank you Jesus, and thank you Richard.*

Alex writes:

> *I have just finished reading this powerful little book and am absolutely thrilled and blown away by its practicality and application. Over the last couple of days in prison ministry, I have prayed for and blessed men in very stressful situations, and seen them lifted and encouraged and hopeful about life. It has also lifted me and equipped me for the prison work and for my own home. **Amidst everything I am encouraged to look for the gold in people** and, if I can't see it, to bless them anyway. Thank you brother.*

That phrase, 'look for the gold in people… and bless them anyway' is an encouragement to us all.

Here's a testimony from Jackie, whose usual habit was to speak demeaning words:

> *I was at church when you preached about* The Awesome Power of Blessing, *and I wanted to tell you what **a profound impact this has had on my life**. I have always had a mouth that rapidly outran my brain, and what came out was often not helpful, kind or pleasant – particularly when I was driving. From the day of the service, I began to pray Jeremiah 15:19 ('…if you take out the precious from the vile, you shall be as My mouth…'), and it has made the most amazing difference. Within about three days, I noticed that it no longer even occurred to me to use those words. I lived in France for some time, so the idea of benediction/malediction was really interesting to me. I realised that my habit was to 'bad speak' over myself and over others. Instead, I began praying over my workplace (a school), and since the children we care for 'live' in this place with us each*

day I prayed the House Blessing. Our school now feels increasingly peaceful and joyful and the children are settled and engaged.

In *The Awesome Power of Blessing*, as Jackie mentioned, I referred to blessing as 'benediction', or good speaking, and cursing as 'malediction' or bad speaking. Here I would like to introduce another word with 'diction' in it – 'jurisdiction' – that is, the territory over which you have a legal right to speak and a legal right to bring under God's dominion. **Your primary jurisdiction is your home.**

Paul writes:

*On Friday, we met a man at the Auckland Promise Keepers ['Believe'] Event who was incredibly impacted by your message, which has **completely changed his thinking**. He said that, as a result, he realised God has called him to be a leader in his home. He's recognising his God-given authority to pray and to bless. His family are not Christians, so instead of talking about his views, he is now blessing his wife and three sons,* *even at the dining table. He said that during dinner there used to be loud negative talk, but in just a week of blessing his family, he is seeing a positive change in the conversation.'*

We all know we have the legal right to decide who and what comes into our home. Which people will you allow, and which will not get past the front door? Shoes on? Yes or no? The dog in? Yes or no?

The same is true in the supernatural realm. Christians have the authority, in Jesus' name, to spiritually bind and loose (which means to forbid or to permit what happens) in the home. What will you bind (forbid)? Sickness, dissension, strife, poverty, demons? What will you permit (loose)? Peace, joy, love, the Kingdom of God? Why not make a list of what you will allow and encourage, and a list of what you will forbid, then speak and declare these intentions over your jurisdiction?

Do you see the importance of the point being made here? I would say that in most cases, people let life 'happen' in their homes. Instead, resolve to speak out in the name of Jesus what will be allowed in the spiritual realm of your home, or not allowed.

Here are two more testimonies from people who, in the course of everyday life, passed the blessing book on to someone else.

David writes:

> *I blessed a friend who is struggling in his marriage over the weekend. I also gave him my copy of the book, which he gratefully accepted. Thank you for writing this book.*

Jude says:

> *I gave your book to a Chinese man here in Vanuatu. He says he has been so blessed with this book. He has even recited the blessings and continues to bless his family. He said that no longer gets angry but instead blesses those around him. Thank you for that little book of powerful and awesome blessings.*

PROSPERING IN BUSINESS OR YOUR PLACE OF WORK

There is no limit to the places that blessing can be used. Your workplace is another area in which you can activate the intentions of God. Below is a transcript from a video sent to me in which Dr Grant Mullen interviews a business owner in New Zealand.

Owner: …*something else that I've come to do more recently is learn about the power of blessing.*

Dr Grant: *How did you come to hear about the power of blessing?*

Owner: *I read a little book by a guy called Richard Brunton,* The Awesome Power of Blessing, *specifically in a business setting, about blessing one's business. So, I started doing that. Each day I have a little alarm that goes off part-*

way through the morning just to remind me, and I pause at my desk and I'll declare God's blessing over the business … 'In the name of Jesus, I bless my business. [Name of business], I bless you in the name of the Father, and the Son and the Holy Spirit. Holy Spirit, I welcome You here,' (just quietly – the other guys don't know that I'm doing it), saying, 'God I need You here in this environment. I declare that Your presence is here, this business is blessed because You're in me and I'm blessing this business.'

And from that we've had some fascinating phone calls where we've landed some of our biggest contracts that have come completely out of the blue. And realising that this declaration of blessing is actually turning into the phone ringing, and business happening, and saying, 'God thank you so much.' I know that it's not me that's doing it. We're working really hard at what we can do, but God is adding that extra amount.

Dr Grant: *So by blessing you're adding a supernatural component to your business?*

Owner: *Yes, certainly, that's what I'm doing and that's what's happening.*

Dr Grant: *Because, as Christians, we have the right to do that and God encourages us to bless. But you've actually proved that it's measurable – you can see the difference in your bottom line – since you've started blessing.*

Now, what would you recommend to the people watching who may be in business, or just working – they don't have to be self-employed, they can be salaried people – what tips would you suggest to change the trajectory of their careers?

Owner: *I'd say it's a matter of pausing and taking that moment to consciously bless the business. Yes, God is with you all the time, but ask for and declare His presence over the room you're in, or the department that you're running and just be active in that. I pray for my team members… 'Lord, give them insights, give them breakthrough, give them ideas they haven't had before.' Just taking a few minutes each day to deliberately do that.*

Dr Grant: That's fantastic. Because we're Christians, we're in a supernatural enterprise. God places us in the business world, and we have every right to use our supernatural tools at work.

A pastor friend of mine took a blessing book with him to the United Kingdom and shared it with a man who wasn't getting on with his boss. This man decided to bless his boss, and did so face to face (which I thought was quite brave). The relationship changed for the better from that point on.

By the way, I hope it's obvious that I don't recommend approaching your boss and saying something like, *'Boss, I bless you in Jesus' name, to listen to your employees more and not talk down to people.'* It's not a good idea to use blessing as a way to confront people!

Better to say:

Boss, I bless you in Jesus' name. I speak God's favour over you, over your family and over your business. I bless your leadership. May God grant our business favour in the client marketplace

and in the employee marketplace. And may God,
by His Spirit, download creative ideas among us
– to improve productivity, and to craft products
and services that would help make our clients
successful. Amen.

Our workplace is not always a business setting. In this next case, it was a school. A friend told me about a discussion he'd had with a schoolteacher who had read the blessing book. He writes:

The schoolteacher was struggling with kids from
low income families, often without fathers at
home, who created havoc in the classroom. He
has been absolutely amazed at the turnaround
as he has applied the principles of blessing. He
also blesses his own kids at home, and now they
won't leave without their blessing for the day.

Perhaps your workplace is a church. Bishop Michael from Kenya says:

One pastor tells me that he often grumbled
because of the small offering the congregation

gave on Sundays, but when he started blessing the congregation with regards to their income, the offering has increased, and the small congregation is now growing bigger.

Pastor Darin from the USA writes:

*I have truly found that what we bless tends to increase (to include relationships, finances and health); so whatever you want to increase, **thank the Lord for what you already have and then start blessing it**. (Instead of grumbling over the lack.)*

Not all of us go out to work in the commercial world or in the community. I like what Bill Johnson says in his book *Dreaming with God*: 'The privilege to be a stay-at-home wife and mother is equal in importance to being a missionary.'

Our homes need blessing. Every responsibility – housework, the grounds outside, food on the table, the way the family talk to each other, the way they value each other, the outworkings of God's destiny in the lives of the parents and the children – everything, when it is blessed intentionally and with faith, can begin to fall into line with God's plan.

LAND BECOMING FERTILE AND PRODUCTIVE

When I think of food shortages in so many parts of the world, I wonder what would happen if Christians moved in faith, in their God-given authority, to break curses off their land and bless it, in the name of Jesus.

Rev. Edward from Uganda writes:

> *My friend has land and trees that were not bearing fruit for years. I gave him* The Awesome Power of Blessing. *He blessed the land and trees, and now they are bearing fruit. He has ordered more books and he is blessing people with them, and great things are happening.*

Pastor Geoff in Northland, New Zealand, says:

> *I was called to pray over a property where it was evident that there were spiritual problems from*

olden times affecting the occupants. The Lord showed me a number of things to cleanse off the land (including attacks and bloodshed), and then I blessed the land to be productive.

The year before, the farm had produced 400 bales of hay. After our blessing, the occupants got 1170 bales when they did their haymaking at the end of the year! This was remarkable, but even more so because there had been a local drought and most people got only half what they'd had the preceding year.

MARRIAGES RESTORED

Whenever I have the opportunity to run a blessing workshop, I ask husbands and wives to bless each other and their children. There is often a moment of awkwardness, even discomfort. Some have difficulty standing face to face, looking each other in the eye, holding hands, and saying such things as, 'I love you, please forgive me.' These moments are often a time of tears and reconciliation that encompass the whole family. I love this ministry of reconciliation.

The photos on the following pages were taken at a blessing workshop in Central Africa.

Many leaders in nations across Africa have taken the message of blessing to heart and are passing it on to their congregations.

Bishop Michael from Kenya says:

*Blessing in Central Africa. Children blessing parents,
parents blessing children, and husbands and wives
blessing each other.*

I have had seminars and crusades in Burundi about the Awesome Power of Blessing. At a seminar I held at Rumonge on the outskirts of Bujumbura, I asked husbands and wives and families to bless each other publicly, and the church was filled with amazement. A man gave a testimony of how his daughter was healed of a migraine after blessing her. Thank you for being a blessing to Africa.

This was written to Pastor Sammy from the Democratic Republic of Congo, and shared with me:

I am so happy to have been blessed by your visit to Togo. I needed it. God has blessed His people with this blessing book. We had a lady whose marriage was a battleground for over two years and was on its way to breaking up. When she received the blessing book, she read it. Her husband noticed that she was engrossed in it and, in her absence, he took the book and read it too. Then when she came back, he asked her if she could get him a copy of the book as well.

We gave her twelve more copies. From then on, there was peace and reconciliation in the marriage. She gives God the glory.

Rev. Edward from Uganda writes:

We did an Awesome Blessing ministry in Apac in Northern Uganda, and lives were blessed and there were many amazing testimonies. One was about a family and marriage that was restored…

Pastor David in Zambia says:

God is doing a lot of work in married couples, and when we pray for blessing for them, they start crying and the Lord creates unity in their lives.

Recently, at a church meeting in New Zealand, I asked how many of the approximately 40 people in attendance had said 'I love you' to their spouse that day. There was no response. 'Last week?' I asked, and a couple of hands were raised. Too often we neglect the verbal aspect of our love. But the fact is we cannot afford to. Our relationships need frequent strengthening because we have an enemy whose very aim is to divide, devastate and destroy.

I suggest that a blessing of your spouse should include:

1. Affirmation ('I love you,' 'You're special,' etc.)
2. Praise (Appreciate some quality that you admire – be specific!)
3. Forgiveness (Ask for and give it, if necessary.)
4. Impartation (Release something from the Kingdom that your spouse needs, such as peace, joy and wisdom.)

PART TWO:

The Powerful
Effect of a
Parent's Blessing

THE FATHER'S BLESSING

Some years ago, I was doing some reading around the subject of blessing and came across an excellent little book written by Frank Hammond called *The Father's Blessing*. I read it and decided to embrace the message. Frank says:

> *The benefits of a Father's Blessing are far reaching and readily make the difference between success and failure; victory and defeat; happiness and misery in an individual's life.*

He goes so far as to say:

> *The cause for curses in a person's life may be due to the failure of a father to fulfil his responsibility to bless his child.*

The effect of blessing is supernatural; it is the presence and power of the Holy Spirit, producing joy, peace, prosperity and fruitfulness, and providing health, success and protection.

In my ministry, I offer to be an alternative channel by which Father God can give people the blessing they never had. In that moment, I am a substitute, or a spiritual father, so I can bless them as a father.

A typical conversation might go something like this:

Did your father ever lay hands on you and bless you?

No.

God always intended that you receive blessings through your father. May I bless you in his place so that you can have the blessing you missed out on?

Okay.

You need to know that this is the presence and

work of the Holy Spirit. I'm going to speak and release a blessing, but it is the Holy Spirit who does the blessing. You understand? So I'm going to lay hands on you and ask the Holy Spirit to come on you. Is that okay?

Yes.

I have modified Frank Hammond's version of the Father's Blessing – or rather, I've added a lot. I would seldom speak all of what follows, but these words serve as an example of how I might form the blessing.

I ask the Holy Spirit to come on the people or person. If it is a one-on-one situation, having asked their permission, I lay hands on the person (that is, I put my hands on their shoulders; or put a hand on their upper back as I stand to the side). Then I speak:

I love you, my child. You are special. You are a gift from God to me. I thank God for allowing me to be a father to you. I love you and I'm proud of you (or 'I'm here for you, I believe in you').

I ask you to forgive me for the things I've said and done that have hurt you. And for the things I didn't do, and for the words I never said that you longed to hear.

I break and cut off every curse that has followed you as a result of my sins, your mother's sins and the sins of your ancestors. I praise God that Jesus became a curse on the cross that we could come out from under every curse and enter into the blessing.

I bless you with the healing of all wounds of the heart that you have suffered – especially the wound of rejection. In Jesus' name, I take authority over every spirit of rejection, every spirit of fear, the spirit of disappointment, the spirit of worthlessness; and I break the power of every cruel and unjust word spoken over you.

I bless you with overflowing peace, the peace that only the Prince of Peace can give.

I bless your life with fruitfulness – good fruit, abundant fruit and fruit that remains.

I bless you with success. I break every limitation off you in Jesus' name. You are the head and not the tail; you are above and not beneath.

I bless the gifts that God has given you. I call forth your potential. I bless you with wisdom to make good decisions and to develop your full potential in Christ.

I bless you with overflowing prosperity, enabling you to be a blessing to others.

I bless you with spiritual influence, for you are the light of the world and the salt of the earth.

I bless you with depth of spiritual understanding and a close walk with your Lord. You will not stumble or falter, for the Word of God will be a lamp to your feet and a light to your path.

I bless you to see women and men as Jesus did and does.

I bless you to see, draw out and celebrate the gold in people, not the dirt.

I bless you to release God in the workplace – not just to testify, or model good character, but also to glorify God with the excellence and creativity of your work.

I bless you with good friends. You have favour with God and man.

I bless you with abounding and overflowing love, from which you will minister God's comforting grace to others. You are blessed, my child! You are blessed with all spiritual blessings in Christ Jesus. Amen!

During the blessing process, *stay open to the Holy Spirit.* For example, as I've been speaking the blessing to a congregation, sometimes I have felt the need to repent on behalf of men who have abused women in the audience. Sometimes, when I bless an individual, I say such things as 'You're a good son' or 'You're a good daughter', or I feel led to prophesy over the individual's life.

The Father's Blessing has become even more significant for me now that I better understand the last two verses of the Old Testament:

> *Behold I'm going to send you Elijah the prophet before the coming of the great and terrible day of the Lord. He will turn the hearts of the fathers to their children, and the hearts of the children to their fathers (a reconciliation produced by repentance) so that I will not come and strike the land with a curse (of complete destruction). (Malachi 4:5-6 AMP)*

These verses demonstrate that God's end-time strategy is the restoration of the fundamental building block of community and life – the family. He will send the spirit and power of Elijah as a Holy Spirit anointing on fathers, to turn their hearts to the children and the hearts of the children to the fathers. God will raise up spiritual fathers in the church to mentor the 'fatherless'. I believe that this ministry of the Father's Blessing is a forerunner of what is to come.

In addition to receiving an impartation of blessing, I have found that, at the same time, the 'father wound' and other wounds are often healed. The 'father wound' is particularly important. As a result of wounds received through a father's absence, lack of demonstrated love or negative words, rejection enters to amplify and bind us to the pain. This can grow into a stronghold that disengages us from the love of God.

We tend to view God through the same lens through which we view our earthly fathers. Their imperfections – particularly where they failed to love and protect us as they should have – are transposed onto Father God. We can see God as distant, severe, harsh, absent, not having time for us, when in fact the opposite is true. We can feel unworthy and unlovable, and consequently unable to receive God's love, goodness and healing. This is a tragedy because we are designed to be open to God's good gifts.

The most powerful part of the Father's Blessing is contained in the first few lines, starting with 'I love you, my child…' Sometimes I wonder if people even hear the rest – they just feel the love.

In our New Zealand culture, and many others, men have difficulty saying 'I love you'. If you struggle with those words, I challenge you to please just take a breath and say them. I was scared the first time, but I can tell you that the Holy Spirit *will* come and do what you cannot do. Let the power and spirit of Elijah come upon you; let the Holy Spirit anoint you and turn your heart to the children – even adult children and the fatherless.

Remember, even Jesus needed to hear His Father's love and affirmation, at His baptism, before He had done any of His mighty works. Then, at the transfiguration, His father repeated those words to strengthen Him for what lay ahead. If Jesus needed to hear that He was loved, then surely we do as well. Be the mouthpiece to communicate that blessing to the people around you.

Testimonies from Adults Receiving a Father's Blessing

I have spoken the Father's Blessing over several hundred people one-on-one, and many thousands more in gatherings and congregations.

In 2019, I had occasion to deliver the Blessing message to about 40 people at a retreat. I finished by speaking the Father's Blessing over them all. I had barely started to speak the words when a woman began sobbing loudly. When I returned to Auckland, I received an email from her as follows:

> *The Lord has transformed my life since I received the powerful anointing through the ministry of the Father's Blessing. Such a deep cry in my heart – delivered from rejection, abandonment etc. That cry had been there for many years, not understood by me. It's gone now… All that rejection was healed in a moment's time, but the other wonderful thing is that I am hearing the Lord's voice more clearly than in all the years I have walked with Him. I am hearing it for my own life, but also in how to proceed in prayer for*

others – it's amazing! (I am 72 and it's powerfully life-changing!) Thank you for coming to share with us so lovingly.

At a Christian conference, I struck up a conversation with the lady sitting next to me and ended up giving her a copy of *The Awesome Power of Blessing*. She flicked through it, then turned to me and asked me to bless her.

I enquired if her father had ever laid hands on her and blessed her.

'No,' she answered.

I then asked, 'May I do that in his place so that God can give you the blessing that was meant to come through your father?'

She agreed.

I prayed that the Holy Spirit would come on her, explaining that it was all about what God was going to do. Then, the moment I began to speak, she started to cry and her weeping continued to the end of the blessing. About two weeks later, I received the following email:

> *Remember me? I am the Chinese girl who sat next to you in the conference, and you blessed me as a spiritual father. I would like to take this opportunity to thank you for the blessing you said over me. Before the conference, I prayed for three things – one of them was to let my father say ['sorry'] to me as he did very bad things to me which is not what a father should do to a daughter. And God is so amazing he let you sit next to me and say ['sorry'] to me on behalf of my father. That's why I cried so much because I just felt God is so real and He answered my prayers in such an amazing way.*

Recently, I was in Brazil, working with a translator. I had occasion to bless a pastor who had never known his father. I have never seen so many tears from a man, and the hug at the end went on forever.

In New Zealand, I have twice spoken at Promise

Keepers conferences for men, and each time I finished with the Father's Blessing. Paul Subritzky, former director of Promise Keepers NZ, wrote a foreword for *The Awesome Power of Blessing*, in which he said that, on those occasions, *'the impact was immensely powerful and life-changing for many'.*

I remember one man approaching me afterwards and saying, 'I've got a bone to pick with you.'

'Oh,' I said, taken aback, as he was quite a big man, 'and why would that be?'

'You made me cry,' he replied with a smile.

Many a tough-looking male has been reduced to tears by the Father's Blessing.

A couple were talking with me one morning about someone we knew, and the conversation turned to the effect on a person of a 'father wound'. I could see that tears were beginning to form in the woman's eyes, so I told her about the Father's Blessing and offered to do it for her. She agreed.

'What about now?' I asked.

'Yes,' she said.

We moved to a nearby space. She shared that her father was physically violent to her and her sister. As I blessed her, she cried and cried. As she composed herself, more of the story unfolded. Someone known to the family had wanted to sexually abuse her and her sister, but she had been too frightened to tell her dad.

I asked if I could give her a father's hug – I think it was the first time she had experienced such a thing. Her whole body shook and trembled as she wept and wept, and then demons left. She left that time of blessing laughing, loving and smiling freely like never before.

During his earthly ministry, Jesus said that He had come to heal the broken-hearted and set captives free. He's still in the same business, except now He's doing it through believers by the power of the Holy Spirit. We have such a loving and beautiful Saviour who wants to minister through us to a world in pain. Listen to His words of intention:

> *The Spirit of the LORD is upon Me, Because He has anointed Me to preach the gospel to the poor; He has sent Me to heal the broken-hearted, to proclaim liberty to the captives and recovery of sight to the blind, to set at liberty those who are oppressed; to proclaim the acceptable year of the LORD. (Luke 4:18-19)*

Notice that healing the broken heart comes before physical healing.

A man came up for prayer at church. I was part of the ministry team and, after I blessed and hugged him, he said, 'All I ever wanted was a hug from my father.'

After praying for an older woman with advanced cancer, I blessed her. She said how much the blessing had meant to her – her father had never told her he loved her. I'm not saying there was a connection between missing out on those words from her father and her illness, but neither can I say there wasn't.

Here's another email I received after I had spoken at a church:

> *A friend had deep-seated father issues due to the way her father had treated her as a child, to the extent that she was completely fearful of men and would always withdraw when men were around. Especially if there was conflict and raised voices, she would always seek to leave as soon as it was physically possible to do so. You prayed the Father's Blessing at the end of the meeting and afterwards she went up for prayer. When you prayed individually for her, God turned up in such a powerful way that all her fear went, and she has become a totally different person. She has never felt such liberty in her life. Her countenance has completely changed and there is a lightness in her appearance that was not there before.*

This arrived in my email inbox from Fiji:

> *I was in New Zealand last year spending time with my elder brother, who died of cancer. I went*

a couple of times with him to church, and you spoke a Father's Blessing over me. I was overwhelmed by the beautiful, healing love of my Heavenly Father. I sure remember so well crying out so many tears... Thank you so much – that was indeed a breakthrough and may God bless you a hundredfold and use you mightily for His Kingdom...

On one occasion, I spoke at a large church in Northland, New Zealand, and finished with the Father's Blessing. Then, on an impulse, I said I was available for hugs. One by one they came, until we ran out of time. In total, around 20 to 30 dear people came for a hug; maybe half wept. I guess two-thirds were women. I remember one woman saying that she had never had a hug from her father.

When I was in Pakistan at the end of 2018, I gave a short message to a homegroup of around 25 to 30 women. I told them that their calling to be a stay-at-home mother was just as valuable in the Kingdom of God as the calling to be a pastor or an evangelist. Then I blessed them with the Father's Blessing.

I was probably culturally insensitive, but nonetheless offered to hug anyone who wanted a hug. Around a dozen women came forward, many with tears.

Some people receive healing just from reading the Father's Blessing aloud. Here are four such testimonies:

> *I'm in tears, wow, it's amazing! I have been so bitter with my old man [my father] and when I read the Father's Blessing in your book, I felt a sharp piercing in my body and my eyes felt like they were on fire, and all the bitterness left me. Now I'm grateful I have a father and he is alive.*

> *I read out the Father's Blessing. I could hardly get the words out – I just cried and cried and felt the Lord was healing me. My own father had only ever cursed me and spoken negatively over me until the day he died. I somehow felt released.*

> *Thank you so much for writing* The Awesome Power of Blessing. *You call it a little book… it is*

in fact much, much, much bigger on the inside than its physical appearance. The Father's Blessing brought me to tears within the first few words… thank you… I needed that healing.

I was given your little booklet. Interesting that something so small can pack such a punch. I read the Father's Blessing and I cried and cried. I took it for myself, from God. My father has passed, and in later life may have said something like that to me, but certainly not earlier. I shared the same blessing with my mother, who wouldn't have had that said over her either. I bless you, as you have blessed me.

Others Speaking a Father's Blessing over their Children or Spiritual Children

As we have seen, we can speak the Father's Blessing on behalf of another; but nothing is more powerful than a father speaking the blessing over his own child, as these testimonies show:

My daughter and son-in-law prayed the blessing of a father over their children the other night and one of the boys sobbed the whole way through; I believe the prayer will be a turning point for his life.

Our neighbour gave us a few copies of your blessing book and we have been enjoying it so very much and sharing it around our friends and family. At a recent family celebration, my husband read the blessing for children and the whole gathering ended up in joyful tears. Some of our children have asked where they can buy copies. As one son said, 'Wow! This is so wonderful!' Thank you for your book and the inspiration it is giving this family and all those we can share it with.'

I spoke to an older man at church today to whom I had given a copy of the book. He told me how it had blown him away and, as a result, he is speaking a Father's Blessing over each of his adult children, with tears, using the prayer in the book.

I shared and gave a blessing book to a great apostle and evangelist of God. After reading it,

*he told me he has been in ministry a long time
but had not seen this revelation this way. He was
so thankful and went ahead to practise it with
his son with whom there had been no contact for
so many years. After blessing, he reached out to
the boy and he responded. Reconciliation after
so many years. Glory to God.*

Axel, a pastor in Indonesia, distributed *The Awesome Power of Blessing* in Bahasa and spoke the Father's Blessing as he did so. He writes:

*I've never hugged so many men in my life before
– many lives restored. Thank you.*

Another pastor writes:

*My son (a pre-Christian) has just come out of his
room with* The Awesome Power of Blessing *that he's been reading and asks me if I will pray
over him the Father's Blessing. He closes his eyes
and soaks in every word! Wow. Out of nowhere!
The hugs that followed were very special. Thank
you, Lord Jesus.*

Top: Pastor Axel in Indonesia
Bottom: Pastor Sammy in the DRC

THE MOTHER'S BLESSING

As we have seen, the verses at the end of Malachi speak of turning the hearts of the *fathers* to the children. What about the mothers? I believe that, in general, mothers' hearts are already turned to the children. When all is as it should be, nothing on earth compares to the love that a mother has for her child. Nonetheless, the words of love and blessing still need to be spoken, and there are those who long to hear these words from their mother.

Testimonies from Adults Receiving a Mother's Blessing

My women's group of twelve ladies was studying your blessing book. Yesterday we reached the part about the Father's Blessing. We decided that we would read out loud the Father's Blessing as a Mother's blessing. My own mother was a 'good

Christian woman' but determined not to spoil her only child! My tears came, deep and fast, and a lovely 'motherly-shaped' sister enfolded me, and now I think that all the mother stuff that I've been trying to work through has truly been healed. Thank you.

While at a church gathering not long ago, I was asked to say the Father's Blessing over the congregation. At coffee afterwards, a woman came up and told me how life-changing the blessing had been. In the course of conversation, she said that her mother had rejected her. I quickly asked a mature Christian woman to bless her as a mother. The effect was dramatic, and the woman received deliverance from rejection and anger.

Earlier this year, I was having breakfast with my pastor and his wife. As we talked, I mentioned that I would have really liked a Mother's Blessing. The pastor's wife said she would bless me. When she had finished, I sensed that I needed her to ask for my forgiveness. As soon as she did that, I burst into tears and cried for some time. I thought I had long ago forgiven my mum, but a deep wound had remained until this point. It was a reminder to me that we are often unaware of the wounds we carry and their effect on us.

Speaking a Mother's Blessing over Children

Thank you for the Father's Blessing. I had no idea how much I needed it until last night. I arrived home and could not wait to bless my kids with the Father's Blessing (I just gave them a Mother's Blessing, believing it is equally effective coming from a single mother.) Thank you so much, and I bless you from the bottom of my heart.

Your little book reduced me to tears – especially the Father's Blessing over his children. I wept for my two sons who never had this blessing over their lives. As their mother, I am blessing them daily as the Spirit leads me, and it has given me new hope and understanding that we can all become overcomers.

AN EVERYDAY BLESSING

Much of the above is about a one-off blessing using the Father's Blessing or Mother's Blessing as a special event. But it is wonderful to establish a daily or weekly routine for blessing your children. Such a blessing would be shorter and less formal, and would change according to circumstances. Here are the important components:

- Love and affirmation in some form (speak it as you hug the child).
- Praise for who they are. (Be careful here when praising their accomplishments, e.g. academic or sporting achievements, lest they associate your love with their performance. They can grow to be performance-orientated, working *for* love instead of working *from* love.)
- Ask for forgiveness.
- Impart something from the Kingdom of God

(e.g. to grow in wisdom and stature and in favour with God, their teachers and other children).

The following three stories of blessing were all sent to me from the same lady. I include them because they are excellent examples of specific, down-to-earth, practical words; and they got results.

My younger son Jimmy did not start primary school from year one but year two, so his maths and English were behind by two years.

In 2016, I bought the book The Awesome Power of Blessing *and started to practise blessing when I drove him to school. I said to him: 'Jimmy, I bless you in the name of the Father, the Son and the Holy Spirit. I bless you with God's favour, protection, peace, health, joy, wisdom, understanding, knowledge, discernment and insight, and that you will find favour with your teachers and friends. You will always be the head and not the tail, you will be successful in all you do, and you will walk in the light of Jesus. Amen.'*

A few months later, he suddenly told me and my husband that he wanted to be one of the top students in his class and told his class teacher the same thing. He got up early every morning, and asked his dad to teach him maths before school. He practised maths twice a day on his own initiative. Things started to change. At the end of Year 8, his maths was one of the best in his class – he achieved excellence and merit. His English writing also went from two years behind to one year ahead, and he attended a Year 9 English writing class. He is now Year 10 and, as usual, I bless him before he leaves home each morning.

About six months ago, my daughter-in-law told me her children didn't want to eat. They were both below the normal on the New Zealand Children's Growth Chart. So I laid hands on the children's tummies and blessed them. I said: 'Aaron and Abigail, Nana blesses you in Jesus' name. I bless you to have a good appetite; you will enjoy everything your mum cooks for you. And everything you eat will become good nutrition to you. You will be a healthy and happy prince and princess.'

I also blessed them: 'The Lord watches over you, the Lord is your shade at your right hand; the sun will not harm you by day, nor the moon by night, you will lie down and sleep in peace…' (words from Psalms 121 and 4). They now eat well and sleep well.

I often visit my elder son's family to cook dinner for them on the weekend. One day, the Holy Spirit reminded me that I should bless my son's family before I left. Chinese people don't always express their love in front of children, so it's a bit embarrassing to bless them face to face. However, I obeyed the Holy Spirit and started to lay hands on my son and his wife and bless them.

I blessed their marriage, work, finance, relationship and health; that they would have the wisdom from the Holy Spirit to know how to bring up their children; that they would be God's faithful servants and so on. Then one day after I blessed them, I had a thought that I should ask them to bless me. Now it has become a routine. I enjoy the moment we bless each other. We are closer than before; I feel the love among us.

PART THREE:

The Powerful Effect of Blessing the Body

PHYSICAL HEALING

A merry heart does good, like medicine, but a broken spirit dries the bones.

Thus says Proverbs 17:22 in the New King James Version, or as the Passion Translation has it:

A joyful, cheerful heart brings healing to both body and soul, but the one whose heart is crushed struggles with sickness and depression.

'Drying of the bones' speaks of a lack of healthy bone marrow. Marrow is the spongy tissue that fills the inside of your bones. There are two types – red and yellow. Red marrow helps produce blood cells, while yellow marrow helps store fat. As you age, your red marrow is gradually replaced by yellow marrow.

Red bone marrow produces:

- Red blood cells, which work to carry oxygen-rich blood around the body.
- Platelets, which help the blood to clot and prevent uncontrolled bleeding.
- White blood cells, which work to help the body fight off infections.

We know that a broken heart (the great grief that arises from a particular situation or relationship) affects our health – it allows sickness and disease to enter our bodies. Emotional and spiritual wounds affect the health of our body, and healing can come through blessing.

Take time to give thanks for the part of the body that needs healing and speak lovingly and gratefully to it. Yes, *speak to the body part as if it can hear you.* You may wish to research how the body part works, so that your gratitude and appreciation is real, and your blessing can be more specific.

The body responds to words spoken over it. If you have complained about your body, then you need to repent of that. Maybe as a teenager, you hated your body because of acne, you thought you were too thin or too fat, or you thought you were too pale or too dark. Ask God's forgiveness and, in the name of Jesus, break the power of the negative words you spoke over yourself.

Then bless your body in the name of the Father, the Son and Holy Spirit (or simply in the name of Jesus). Doing so releases God's love and power. Healing may take place quickly or slowly. In some of the testimonies that follow, healing came overnight, or took place in a few days or weeks or months. Don't give up.

I regularly pray with people for healing – usually through the laying on of hands, commanding the disease or sickness to go in the name of Jesus, then releasing healing. Sometimes the healing is immediate, sometimes it takes time. On one occasion, I prayed for a woman with endometriosis. It seemed that nothing had happened, but two weeks later her mother testified that the doctor could no longer find evidence of the disorder.

There are times when the healing doesn't come, or it comes but then the ailment returns. Sometimes there are reasons for this, such as unforgiveness or generational and other curses, but I am becoming increasingly convinced that wounds of the heart are often a significant cause as well. For example, demons are usually behind addictions, but if the root is actually a wound of the heart, which allows rejection to enter, and if the root is not dealt with, then demons can return. (I'll discuss wounds of the heart in more detail in Part Four.)

So when I pray for people, I often speak a Father's Blessing over them because it leads to the healing of the heart. If the person isn't healed straight away, I tell them to continue to bless their body on a daily basis and to keep an eye out for healing changes.

Below are several testimonies of physical healing. Some of these healings clearly came as a consequence of first experiencing a healing of the heart. Others simply came from blessing the body – especially the particular body part that needed healing.

Irritable Bowel

I had a long and difficult journey navigating my way through depression. Healing my past was key, with the most significant step forward being to forgive my father – not only for hurtful things he had done, but more so for the things he hadn't done. He couldn't find loving, caring, emotional words to say – despite a craving in my soul to hear them.

Whilst, through this journey, my depression lifted, I still carried some physical symptoms – the worst being irritable bowel syndrome. My doctor had prescribed drugs and a diet to manage the symptoms, but could not provide a lasting remedy.

Richard had been telling me stories about the Father's Blessing, and what responses people had. Something in my spirit caught hold of the idea. While I had forgiven my father for the gap he left, I hadn't actually filled that gap or satisfied my soul's craving.

And so it happened. Richard stepped into the shoes of my father and blessed me as a son. The Holy Spirit fell on me and remained with me that entire day. It was a beautiful experience and that part of my soul which had been crying out was at peace.

An unexpected outcome, however, was that my symptoms of irritable bowel syndrome stopped completely. My medication and the doctor's diet were thrown out. When my soul received what it had been craving, my body was healed too.

Chest Pain

On one occasion, I released a Father's Blessing over a beautiful woman of God. Several people were trying to deliver her of something – a pain in her chest I think – but they ran out of time and asked me to take over. 'Did your father ever lay hands on you and bless you?' I asked.

'I know that he loved me,' she replied defensively.

'But did he bless you?'

'No,' she replied.

'May I bless you in his place?'

'Yes,' she said.

From the moment I began the blessing with the words 'I love you' until the end, the tears came from her like a flood. She cried so much that there was a big wet patch on the carpet. We were both shocked at her reaction. The chest pain disappeared, but she had received much more than a physical healing.

Deaf Ear

I was sitting in a meeting when the leader discerned that I should speak a Father's Blessing over a particular woman. Midway through the blessing, she suddenly exclaimed, 'I can hear! I can hear!' Unbeknown to me, she had been deaf in one ear, and was now healed.

Panic Attack

I was in my mid-twenties when I started to wake at night with horrible episodes of my heart racing for no reason, and something beneath my chest would churn like a ball. My face and limbs would go numb and tingly, then I would start to shake. Each time I thought I was dying, or about to die. Tests at the hospital showed nothing. A year later, a chiropractor told me it was likely anxiety attacks. This came as a surprise, as I didn't think I was an anxious person.

I was sceptical when you (Richard) talked about the power of blessings. I was well out of my comfort zone when you asked us to bless the person behind. Then, when you asked us to raise our hands to receive the Father's Blessing, I squirmed, but I did it anyway as everyone else was. So I raised my arms for the first time in church.

I think you were about one sentence into the Father's Blessing when I felt something begin to happen. First, there was a sudden emotional response and my eyes started welling up. I tried to stop crying. Then an anxiety attack came out of nowhere, as strong as I'd ever felt it in a way that had never happened before. Never having experienced one during the day before, I thought, 'Oh no, this is not good.' I was scared and hoped you would stop talking so it would go away.

But just then, I felt something very palpable, very 'wave-like' hit me and move right through me from front to back. That churning ball of what-ever it was inside me dissolved instantly – gone without a trace. In fact, looking back, I feel the anxiety flared up almost as if it knew what was about to happen and sought to resist, but was destroyed anyway, and amazingly with such ease by this force. I know now that it was the Spirit of God healing me because I have not had one of those attacks since that day. They stopped completely. And that was years ago now.

So, I just want to say a big thank you. I am clearly a believer in blessings now. I often wonder why God healed me that day, given my poor attitude. I was the least deserving person in the entire congregation. But it was like God said, 'You don't want my blessing… too bad… I'm going to give it to you anyway. Here it is.' We serve a very great and wonderful God.

Chronic Back Pain

Bishop E from Apac in Northern Uganda writes:

One of the ladies we ministered to had severe back pain and could not walk; she was just carried around; the doctors had treated her but given up. After the ministry, and having read the book, she forgave those who had offended her and started to bless them and bless her body also. Immediately the pain left, and she wanted to go to the beach.

Large Mass on Adrenal Gland

Pastor Craig writes:

Last year I went for an ultra-sound scan for a pain in my groin/testicle. Not finding anything, the specialist thought to check my kidneys. She found a large mass on my adrenal gland, and I was sent to another specialist who said there was a chance it could be cancer (the mass measured six centimetres).

My wife said to the specialist, 'Thank you, but we do not accept that,' and I agreed. I am a man devoted to prayer, an itinerant pastor and a man of faith, and have had the privilege of seeing incredible signs and wonders of the Lord's power. (But I admit it feels different when the person facing a personal giant is me!)

It was then that I read just a small section of The Awesome Power of Blessing *and my first thought was, 'This will do.' I started blessing my adrenal gland and researched its function. I continued to bless it every morning as well as the hormones it released and what it was meant to be doing in my body.*

Month by month, test by test, the journey continued. Believe me when I say I had some ups and downs on this road. Finally we got a follow-up appointment to meet the specialist again. She said, 'Well, I only have good news for you! All the scans and reports have come back, and they simply cannot find the mass!' We shared with the doctor our faith and belief in a God who can do miracles like this. Praise the Lord for all He has done!

Since then we have shared this testimony and seen even more miracles! For example, a lady whose ankle was in continuous pain with very little movement – due to a metal rod and four pins – gained full movement with all pain gone after a few simple prayers. In conclusion, the power of blessing works!'

Endocrine Disorder and Thumb Nail Injury

Having been under specialist care for 20 years, I was really drawn to the part in your book about blessing our bodies. I immediately launched into praying blessings and felt a marked improvement. My specialist has been amazed at my progress. In his career as an endocrinologist, he has seen only two people make it to the level of healing I have achieved.

I was feeling so good I decided to do some gardening. Unfortunately, I snagged my thumb and a huge part of my nail came away. I quickly cleaned the area, but my thumb was raw and angry. I placed my other hand around it and thanked it for functioning so well up until now. God reminded me of what this small, unassuming part of my body had done – cared for people, baked for charities, planted trees, played instruments and sports. Then like a wellspring, I uttered, 'Thumb, may you be blessed in your God-given capability to heal; may this pain and infection leave. May my good hand become that of Christ.' I then felt an intense heat from my good hand flood the wounded one, and even a slight pulse, which at first frightened me. I quickly let go then felt God say, 'Would you just trust me?' I did, so I prayed again the next day. Then, on the third day, I saw that my thumb was healed.

Ovarian Cysts

A few weeks ago, my friend had a scan which confirmed that she had ovarian cysts. In excruci-

ating pain one morning, she remembered what she had read from your book and then began to bless her ovaries. The pain went, and a subsequent scan shortly after showed that the cysts had disappeared. She then realised the power of blessing and rang me to testify.

Sore Back

A friend came to visit my wife and me one day. She suffered from a bad back and it had kept her in bed the previous week. She wasn't a Christian, but I asked if I could pray for her to be healed. She agreed, having seen Facebook posts about my ministry. I felt to ask her, 'You never knew your father did you?'

'No,' she answered.

I explained the Father's Blessing then began it. As we hugged, my right hand was on her back and I released healing in Jesus' name. Then I asked her, 'Would you like to meet the Healer?'

She said, 'You mean Jesus, don't you?

'Yes. Would you like to meet Jesus?'

'Okay.'

I led her in a prayer to accept Jesus. She was wonderfully born again.

Lung Nodule
Pastor John from Tanzania sent me this testimony from one of his blessing seminars:

> *A successful businessman had pain in his chest and difficulty breathing. An x-ray, which was done in India, showed that he had a cancerous nodule. Together with his wife they blessed his body, health and lungs. The doctor had said healing was impossible, so they blessed him too. Two months later, they went to a cancer specialist in India who took another scan. No sign of cancer and no pain. Amazement and many tears. All the glory to Jesus Christ.*

Alcohol Addiction
A pastor who attended a conference in Kenya heard

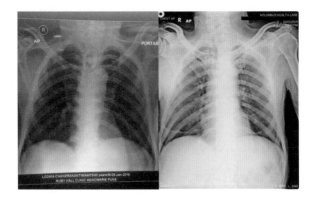

Before and after – disappearing cancer

the blessing message, then preached it in his church the following Sunday. He had this to say:

> *Many testimonies are coming in since the Sunday service. Sister Rose, a member of the church, was married to an alcoholic husband. We prayed for the husband for over five years, but the drinking habit worsened. But when I preached how to bless on Sunday, Sister Rose blessed her husband and he has not drunk alcohol since.*

Over the last few years, I have seen a number of testimonies about the powerful effect of a wife blessing an alcoholic husband. Glory to God who breaks the chains of addiction.

Nicotine Addiction

Our son (a pre-Christian) has been smoking for over ten years. It is a huge cost to his family and he keeps saying he wants to quit. After reading your book, I started blessing him with freedom from nicotine addiction. He was going through a bit of financial stress and he phoned me to say he really wanted to stop smoking, especially as his two children were ['at him'] to quit. I prayed with him over the phone that God would give him the strength and willpower to stop, then blessed him with the freedom from nicotine addiction! Anyway, a few days later, he phoned again to say he had stopped smoking that same night, and hadn't wanted a cigarette since. Amen, thank you Lord.

Witchdoctor Converted; Diabetes Healed

Pastor John, from Tanzania, reported that he had run a blessing seminar attended by many Catholic and Lutheran leaders. In the town, there was a witch-doctor who would curse and put spells on people, including Christian leaders, and especially a particular Catholic bishop and his family. The bishop read *The Awesome Power of Blessing* and decided to give a copy to the witchdoctor. He did so and blessed the man as he presented him with the book. In brief, the witchdoctor is now a born-again Christian.

Another man, who attended the same seminar, had diabetes and needed an insulin injection every day. He decided to bless his body and blood sugar levels. Within days, he had a blood test and was told he could cease the injections!

Herniated Disc

> *After reading* The Awesome Power of Blessing, *my daughter and I were galvanised into action. The first healing I was involved in after reading your book, was with a lady who had a herniated*

disc. You could actually feel the jelly out of alignment in the spine. She was bent over and in great pain. I asked the Holy Spirit for guidance on how to pray. He encouraged me to pray for the spine to come into alignment and for every sinew, atom of her being, blood vessel and ligament to be blessed in the name of the Father, Jesus Christ His Son, and the Holy Spirit. I blessed all the work of her hands, and spoke every other blessing that came to mind during the prayer. As I prayed, I felt really strong heat in my right hand over the spine.

Two weeks later, the lady told me she had been healed that Sunday and had not had a painkiller since. At the time of the prayer, she had felt no immediate improvement or the heat I had felt. However, four hours after the prayer, she realised she was completely healed and pain-free.

Bone Ailments

Pastor John, in Tanzania, writes:

Last weekend I ran a blessing seminar in a Muslim area and spoke to about 70 people who had converted to Christianity. I began by breaking curses off them, then asked them to forgive and bless those who have hurt or cursed them in the past. Then I asked the people to bless the health and well-being of someone else in the group and also to receive from them such a blessing. Afterwards, I asked for testimonies.' Many people came up the front to testify of healing – especially of bones. *'I don't touch them myself; they are just as qualified as I am.'*

Chronic Pain

Bishop Edward Baleke writes:

A lady was suffering with a severe condition and was always in pain. She had been praying, ['God heal me and take away the pain,'] but it persisted. After reading The Awesome Power of Blessing, *she decided to bless her body instead. She was healed totally and is now well.*

Stomach Ulcer and Skin Allergy

It was in November 2019, when I attended the

Gathering of Generals pastors' conference in Turbo, Kenya, that I met Bishop Edward Baleke from Uganda and Sammy Nduwayo from the Democratic Republic of Congo. They were speaking about The Awesome Power of Blessing. *I was seriously suffering from a stomach ulcer and skin allergy. After the session, I went back to the hotel and blessed my body. Next morning, I was miraculously healed. I went to buy a copy of the book for myself and was given the last one available. I have already read it twice and have prepared a sermon to preach this Sunday.'*

Skin Lesions

For the past four years, I have had three lesions on my back. They were ugly, but not cancerous, and the doctor would not remove them. I blessed my skin for several nights and was expecting them to disappear. I could not reach them to scratch them off, and my husband refused to do anything to them either. They appeared to be growing in size and looked worse. One day, my daughter was putting sunscreen on my back and she said to me, 'I feel like I want to scratch at these growths on your back – is that okay?' I told her to go ahead and, although she has very short fingernails, the first one just popped off in her hand. She went ahead and removed the other two as well. The wonderful thing for me is there is no scarring from them, and I no longer have to see them in a place I cannot reach.'

Another testimony about the healing of skin comes from a man named David, who wrote:

As I blessed my skin, pre-cancerous lumps on my arms have disappeared!

Bone Pains and Deaf Ear
From Zambia:

When we pray blessings for people, they are freed from demons and they also recover from bone pains and receive the Holy Spirit. Through the message of The Awesome Power of Blessing, *many people are accepting Jesus Christ. Two weeks ago, we prayed and blessed a young deaf boy and now he can hear. Glory to the Lord! Through the message of* The Awesome Power of Blessing *many people are accepting Jesus Christ. Many also agreed to water baptism after reading the book.*

Persistent Cough

Praise the Almighty Lord Jesus. I cannot stay silent because your book has changed my life. I had a continual cough and, after many examinations at hospital in vain, I decided to practise the theory of blessing my body. What a surprise – after five days, the cough was gone! Also, that day I decided to bless my beautiful daughters, and I learnt to forgive and forget what happened between me and my wife. Truly the practice of blessing can change our world.

Haemorrhoids

Pastor Israel, in the Democratic Republic of Congo, writes:

The blessing message has had an impact on my spiritual life. I can't finish talking to someone without blessing them. I also have a testimony about healing of haemorrhoids after blessing my health. Before, I couldn't work through the evening without being exhausted; now I can. Thanks to Almighty God. Now I am teaching the big, powerful message of blessing.

Brain Injury Trauma

The Awesome Power of Blessing *has changed me at my core – it has changed what I think about as I wake up, my attitude to my body and illness, and it is changing my family and friends. My friend Mary and I break bread most days and bless ourselves and everyone in our sphere, including my cousin whom I care for. He had a brain injury and other injuries to his left side after being run down by a car six years ago. He has been very verbally and physically aggressive from trauma, but now he is changing every day. He is less aggressive and more in his right mind.*

Weight Problems

After reading The Awesome Power of Blessing, *I decided to put it to trial. I started speaking blessing over myself. This may sound strange, but I started blessing myself with weight loss and blessing myself as a thinner man. So far I have lost 37 kilos because, after a few weeks of speaking blessing over myself, I knew I had a shift in the way I was thinking and felt I was in the right frame of mind to commit to a programme. Not finished yet but nearly at goal weight!*

Vision Problems

One gentleman no longer needs to wear glasses as his wife has been blessing his eyes to see. Praise the Lord.

Coma

I was told about a man who had been in a coma for two months after suffering a serious head injury in an accident. His wife had been to a blessing seminar and decided to come into the hospital every day to bless her husband. After about twelve days, the man opened his eyes and can now move his hands. Hallelujah. They are very excited. Many Muslims who attended the seminar are testifying of healings too. Praise God, who releases His healing power when we speak blessing in faith, and love, and thanksgiving, in the mighty name of Jesus.

PART FOUR:

The Powerful Effect of Blessing a Wounded Heart

HEALING THE HEART

Until I began to speak the Father's Blessing over people, I hadn't given much thought to wounds of the heart.

Everyone suffers from these wounds to some degree. We live in a broken world, with broken people, and when we haven't received love, we struggle to pass it on or know how to love others properly. We have all, to some extent, experienced the pain that comes when someone who should have loved us did not. These wounds affect our lives, and our relationship with God and the people around us.

Psalm 147:3 tells us that God *'heals the broken-hearted and binds up their wounds'.*

When Jesus began His ministry, He spoke these words from the Book of Isaiah:

The Spirit of the LORD is upon Me,
Because He has anointed Me To preach the
gospel to the poor;
He has sent Me to heal the broken-hearted,
To proclaim liberty to the captives
And recovery of sight to the blind,
To set at liberty those who are oppressed;
To proclaim the acceptable year of the LORD.
(Luke 4:18-19 NKJV, emphasis added)

I believe that healing the broken heart is a higher priority than physical healing and deliverance. As mentioned in Part Three, in many cases a wound of the heart – and the anger, resentment and fear that often come with it – can lead to sickness and allow an entry point for the demonic realm.

In Part Two, I explained how the Father's and Mother's Blessing can heal wounds of the heart – especially a wound that comes about through the actions (or inaction) and words (or silence) of our father or mother. But our parents are not the only ones who can wound us. Others may have spoken cruel and unjust words over us that have had a lasting impact – especially if those words were spoken when we were young.

It is not my intention to examine the ins and outs of the wounds of the heart in detail here, but if you are interested in exploring the subject further, I recommend *Exposing the Rejection Mindset* by Mark DeJesus.

I personally suffered a lot of rejection in my childhood and youth, and much of it came from the fact that I didn't seem to fit in. My mother made me wear round-toed, practical shoes when the other lads had pointy ones. I had short hair when the fashion was to have it long. Plus, I was tall and lanky. You get the picture! I know others have been through much worse, but these things were enough to have a lasting impact.

About three years ago, I developed a routine for healing the wounds of my heart. I have included this method of blessing below, hoping that it will help some of my readers.

Note: If the wound event is highly traumatic and revisiting it would take you to a dark place, then I strongly suggest that you see a Christian counsellor, rather than undertaking the following process alone.

1. Identify the wound event – your memory of being wounded. If a particular person wounded you multiple times, I have found it's better to deal with the major events separately rather than as a group.

2. Identify and name the pain – was it rejection, humiliation, injustice, shame, grief or something else?

3. Speak out the pain to God with full emotion. The Book of Psalms is full of raw emotion, so don't be afraid to be emotionally honest with God.

4. Forgive the one who hurt you.

5. Bless the one who hurt you.

6. Ask Jesus to take away the pain, believe He has done that, and thank Him for it.

7. Cast out any spirit that has taken advantage of your pain, as it no longer has a right to be there.

8. Ask God to fill you with His loving acceptance. Receive it and thank Him for it.

9. Revisit the wound event in your imagination.

10. If there is still pain, repeat the process until the wound is completely healed.

11. Take time to consider what outcomes the wound has had in your life. Sometimes, we may have accepted the wounds and let them define us. For example, because someone once said you were 'useless', you may have taken that idea to heart and owned it. Over time it may have become part of your self-identity. If this is true for you, repent and break every agreement you have made with a lie.

12. Speak the truth over yourself: God created you, so you are well-made; He has a destiny for you and you are not 'useless' to fulfil it; and, even

though people speak and act out of their own flawed hearts, God's Word is the Truth.

A Real Life Example

Here's an example of how I have used this healing method in every day life:

I'm looking back to a wound event from childhood. I was probably around ten or eleven years old. My father took me fishing up the Mohaka river in Hawke's Bay, New Zealand. I was yet to catch my first trout. Dad stood back and gave me first shot at each new pool, waiting and watching as I cast my line. Finally, around early afternoon, I succeeded! I proudly examined the trout. At last, I was the man! I had passed into manhood!

My father's response, however, was, 'Thank goodness that's done. Now I can get on with my fishing.' Then off he went (or, at least, that's how I remember it). All of a sudden, I wasn't 'the man'; I felt like a nuisance. I thought my dad wanted me there, but perhaps taking me along was just a duty to be fulfilled.

Sitting now in the present, with my remembered pain, I tell God how I felt. I felt I was a nuisance. Of little value. Dad didn't have time for me. I felt he was harsh and a bit scary.

I forgive my father. Then I bless him. I can see that he'd probably worked hard all week; it had been his day off and he'd taken me with him. I can now see things from his point of view. I bless him in Jesus' name, to prosper, to know God, to work without feeling burdened, to enjoy his latter years.

I pray, 'Jesus, you came to heal my wounds. My spirit, my joy was crushed that day. Please take away the pain, in your name, Lord. I receive it now by faith. Thank you, Jesus.'

I cast out of my being every spirit of rejection, fear of rejection, self-rejection, and the spirit of worthlessness, simply by telling them to go in the name of Jesus. I break every agreement I've made with Satan's lies, in the name of Jesus.

What were the consequences of the wound? I never

really had a close relationship with my father. I think that has impacted me as an adult and affected how I saw Father God. I had pictured God as severe, too busy to have time for me. I wasn't good enough. Lies. The truth is that I am the 'apple of God's eye'. He passionately loves me. Like the father in the story of the prodigal son, He ran to me when I turned to Him when I was filthy and desperate. He cleaned me up, put a ring on my finger, killed the fattened calf and threw a joyful party!

I continue, 'Fill me, Lord, with Your beautiful Spirit. Thank you. Take away every barrier to receiving Your love. Reveal to me the love of the Father as a personal experience. Fill me with His love. Thank you, Lord. I receive it now.'

Now I revisit the wound event in my imagination. Is there still some pain there? If not – I'm free of the wound that has held me back! If some remains, then I repeat the process until all pain is gone. It works and it is life-changing.

BECOMING
LOVE MACHINES

Having the wounds of our heart healed transforms us into more loving people – people who can receive love, pass it on and be less likely to wound the people around us. In many ways, this is the core of the blessing message. We are to become love machines!

Here is part of one of St Paul's famous prayers:

*And may you, having been [deeply] rooted and [securely] grounded in love, be fully capable of comprehending with all the saints (God's people) the width and length and height and depth of His love [**fully experiencing** that amazing, endless love]; and [that you may come] to know [practically, through **personal experience**] the love of Christ which far surpasses [**mere**] **knowledge** [**without experience**], that you may be filled up [throughout your being] to all the fullness of God* *[so that you may have the **richest experience** of God's presence in your lives, completely filled and flooded with God Himself]. (Ephesians 3:17b-19 AMP, emphasis added)*

When we know, by personal experience, how much God loves us, everything changes.

PART FIVE:

The Language
of Blessing

HOW TO CONSTRUCT A BLESSING

The ability to bless is a wonderful gift that is open to us all as children of God. You'll begin to see all kinds of situations where blessing can have a lasting and positive effect. But it takes practice. At first, many people struggle with finding the right words to say, and simply revert to the phrase, 'God bless you.'

As often as possible, when I give the blessing message, I also run a practical blessing workshop afterwards. The following is a summary of my coaching from those sessions, which provides a guide for how to construct a blessing.

In all cases, start with:

I BLESS YOU, in the name of the Father, and of the Son, and of the Holy Spirit… (or, I BLESS YOU in the name of Jesus…)

Then use one or more of the following starting words: MAY, TO, WITH, I RELEASE…

Let's start with examples of using the word 'MAY':

I BLESS YOU, in the name of the Father, and of the Son, and of the Holy Spirit…

MAY God give you a revelation of how much He loves you and rejoices over you.

MAY all of God's plans and purposes for your life come to pass.

MAY the love of God surround you and fill you, and may you know in the deepest part of your being how much he adores and rejoices over you.

MAY you become fully the man/woman of God, the husband/wife and the father/mother that God always planned for you to be.

Now let's use 'TO':

I BLESS YOU, in the name of the Father, and of the Son, and of the Holy Spirit…

TO be strong and courageous.

TO fully comprehend the authority you have in Christ Jesus to release the Kingdom wherever you go.

TO know in the deepest part of your being how much God loves you and watches over you.

Now 'WITH':

I BLESS YOU, in the name of the Father, and of the Son, and of the Holy Spirit…

WITH overflowing peace.

WITH abounding love.

WITH health and strength of body, soul and spirit.

And finally, 'I RELEASE':

> *I BLESS YOU, in the name of the Father, and of the Son, and of the Holy Spirit…*

> *I RELEASE God's love and power in all the circumstances of your life.*

> *I RELEASE God's healing power to flow through your body.*

> *I RELEASE ideas from the Kingdom of Heaven to improve productivity in your business.*

Blessing a Situation

If you are addressing a situation, rather than an individual person, the wording will need to be different. For example:

> *I bless this situation of dispute between (person A) and (person B), in Jesus' name. By doing this, Lord, I believe I am enabling/releasing You to move in the situation to move it from where it is now to where you want it to be. I let go of my*

own agenda, Lord; may your will be done. LET THERE BE a just outcome. LET THERE BE reconciliation. I release the situation into your hands, Lord. Thank you. Amen.

Blessing a Stranger or Someone You Don't Know Well

When you minister to a stranger or someone you don't well, make sure you build rapport, even briefly, so that they don't think you're weird. Make conversation. Always be wise, respectful and kind.

Then ask if you could speak a short blessing over them. If they are agreeable, speak something inoffensive, but powerful nonetheless, like this:

I bless you in the name of Jesus.

May all of God's plans and purposes for your life come to pass.

I release His love and power in all the situations of your life.

And may you know, in the deepest part of your being, how much He loves you.

In Jesus' name, Amen.'

If the person is open, then expect the Holy Spirit to give you more. All this comes with practice and as you mature in the gift. Remember, always keep love and the best interests of the person as your primary focus. Great things can happen!

Final Word

A BLESSING

I would like to finish by blessing you, dear brother or sister in Christ.

I bless you, in the name of Jesus, to be conscious always of the Kingdom of God within you.

I bless you to speak and release the Kingdom wherever you go, in the authority you have in Christ Jesus.

Be stirred up. The King wants to minister through you.

Be moved by His love and compassion to bless others.

And enter into His joy as you do so.

Now, if you would like to, may I suggest that you stand and speak this same blessing over yourself.

Then, as James 4:8 says, '*Draw near to God and He will draw near to you.*' As a prophetic action, I suggest you take a physical step forward into the presence and love of God, with hands outstretched, and simply receive.

Love and blessings.

HOW TO BECOME
A CHRISTIAN

This little book was written for Christians. By 'Christians', I don't just mean people who live good lives. I mean people who are 'born again' by the Spirit of God and who love and follow Jesus Christ.

People are made in three parts: spirit, soul and body. The spirit part was designed to know and commune with a holy God, who is Spirit. Humans were made for intimacy with God, spirit to Spirit. However, human sin separates us from God, resulting in the death of our spirit and loss of communion with God.

Consequently, people tend to operate out of their souls and bodies only. The soul comprises the intellect, the will and the emotions. The result of this is only too apparent in the world: selfishness, pride, greed, hunger, wars, and lack of true peace and meaning.

But God had a plan to redeem humankind. God the Father sent His Son, Jesus, who is also God, to come to earth as a man to show us what God is like – *'if you have seen Me you have seen the Father'* – and to take upon Himself the consequences of our sin. His horrible death on the cross was planned from the very beginning and was predicted in detail in the Old Testament. He paid the price for humankind's sin. Divine justice was satisfied.

But then God raised Jesus from the dead. Jesus promises that those who believe in Him will also be raised from the dead to spend eternity with Him. He gives us His Spirit now, as a guarantee, so that we would know Him and walk with Him for the remainder of our earthly lives.

So, there we have the essence of the gospel of Jesus Christ. If you acknowledge and confess your sin, if you believe that Jesus took your punishment upon Himself on the cross and that He was raised from the dead, then His righteousness will be imputed to you. God will send His Holy Spirit to regenerate your human spirit – that's what it means to be born again –

and you will be able to begin to know and commune with God intimately – which is why He created you in the first place! When your physical body dies, Christ will raise you up and give you a glorious, imperishable one. Wow!

While you continue on this earth, the Holy Spirit (who is also God) will work in you (make you new inside and more like Jesus in character) and through you, to be a blessing to others.

Those who choose not to receive what Jesus paid for will go to judgement with all its consequences. You don't want that.

Here is a prayer you can pray. If you pray it sincerely you will be born again.

Dear God in heaven, I come to You in the name of Jesus. I acknowledge to You that I am a sinner. (Confess all your known sins.) I am truly sorry for my sins and the life that I have lived without You, and I need Your forgiveness.

I believe that Your only Son, Jesus Christ, shed His precious blood on the cross and died for my sins, and I am now willing to turn from my sin.

You said in the Bible (Romans 10:9) that if we declare that Jesus is Lord and believe in our hearts that God raised Jesus from the dead, we shall be saved.

Right now I confess Jesus as the Lord of my soul. I believe that God raised Jesus from the dead. This very moment I accept Jesus Christ as my own personal Saviour and, according to His Word, right now I am saved. Thank you, Lord, for loving me so much that You were willing to die in my place. You are amazing, Jesus, and I love You.

Now I ask You to help me by Your Spirit to be the person that You purposed for me to be from before the beginning of time. Lead me to fellow believers and the church of Your choice that I might grow in You. In Jesus' name, Amen.

Thanks for reading this little book.
I would love to receive testimonies of how
blessing has transformed your life, or the lives
of those you've blessed.

Please contact me via:
richard.brunton134@gmail.com

Visit
www.richardbruntonministries.org

Other Books by Richard Brunton

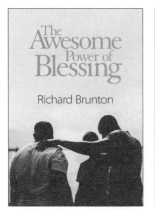 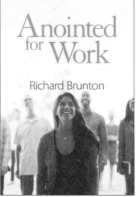

The bestselling *Awesome Power of Blessing* has been translated into over 35 languages and well over one million copies have been printed. In this small book, you will find out how blessing works and learn how to bless the people and situations around you.

Anointed for Work is an invitation to step into an exciting and fulfilling world, where the supernatural has a powerful impact in the workplace.